Henry Purcell

COME, YE SONS
OF ART, AWAY

(ODE FOR QUEEN MARY'S BIRTHDAY, 1694)

for Soprano, 2 Counter-tenor (Alto) and Bass soloists,
SATB chorus and orchestra

**Words probably by
NAHUM TATE**

**Edited by
BRUCE WOOD**

Vocal Score

Order No: NOV 072467

NOVELLO PUBLISHING LIMITED

Editor's Note

This vocal score is uniform with a new edition of the full score, included in Purcell Society Volume 24, which results from a critical appraisal of all sources of the music. Previous editions, prepared by Geoffrey Shaw (1926) and by Michael Tippett and Walter Bergman (1951), appear to have relied exclusively on the only *complete* source (London, Royal College of Music, MS 993), a late 18th-century copy which is frequently defective and occasionally quite corrupt.

The editorial policy followed here conforms to that in the full score, which contains a full explanation of it. In particular, accidentals not found in the sources (including cautionary accidentals) are printed in small type; in the keyboard reduction, however, accidentals which are necessitated solely by the compression of two or more parts onto a single stave are printed full size. Also printed in small type are the continuo realization, which is wholly editorial, and a few bars which have been editorially emended in their entirety (for example, the penultimate bar of the counter-tenor part). Slurs and ties not found in the sources are crossed; other markings and directions supplied by the Editor are enclosed within square brackets.

Orchestral material uniform with this edition is available on hire from the publishers.

BRUCE WOOD
University of Wales: Bangor
December 1997

© Copyright 1997 Novello & Company Limited.

Published in Great Britain by Novello Publishing Limited
Head office: 14/15 Berners Street, London W1T 3LJ

Sales and Hire: Music Sales Distribution Centre,
Newmarket Road, Bury St Edmunds, Suffolk IP33 3YB
Tel. 01284 702600   Fax 01284 768301

Web: www.chesternovello.com   e-mail: music@musicsales.co.uk

COME, YE SONS OF ART, AWAY

(Ode for Queen Mary's birthday, 1694)

Edited by
BRUCE WOOD

HENRY PURCELL

[SYMPHONY]
Largo

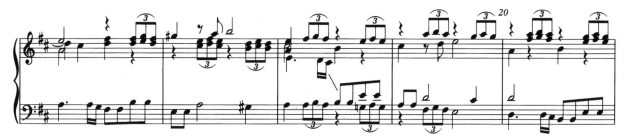

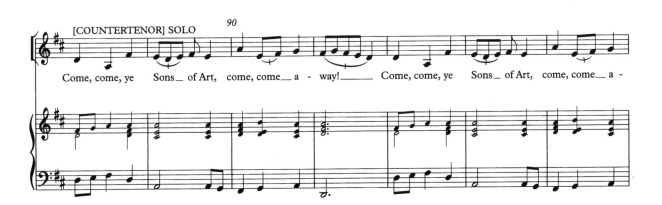

[COUNTERTENOR] SOLO

Come, come, ye Sons_ of Art, come, come_ a - way!_____ Come, come, ye Sons_ of Art, come, come_ a -

4

135

Tune all__ your voi - ces,__ and__ in - stru - ments play, To ce - le - brate, to ce - le - brate this

Tune all__ your voi - ces,__ and in - stru - ments play, To ce - le - brate, to ce - le - brate this

Tune all____ your voi - ces, and in - stru - ments play, To ce - le - brate, to ce - le - brate this

Tune all your voi - ces, and in - stru - ments play, To ce - le - brate, to ce - le - brate this

140

tri - um - phant day, To ce - le - brate, to ce - le - brate this tri - um - phant day.

tri - um - phant day, To ce - le - brate, to ce - le - brate this tri - um - phant day.

tri - um - phant day, To ce - le - brate, to ce - le - brate this tri - um - phant day.

tri - um - phant day, To ce - le - brate, to ce - le - brate this tri - um - phant day.

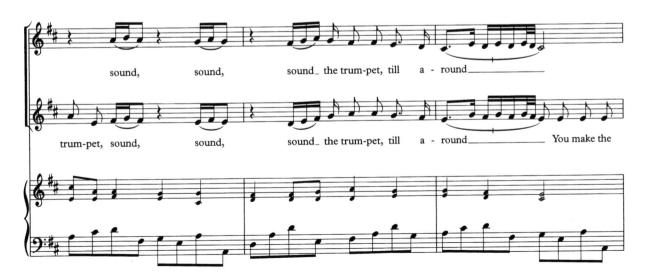

ies of this day; day.

glor - - - ies of this day; On the day.

in - struments play, To ce - le-brate, to ce - le-brate this tri - um - phant day;

in - stru - ments play, To ce - le-brate, to ce - le-brate this tri - um - phant day;

in - stru-ments play, To ce - le-brate, to ce - le-brate this tri - um - phant day;

in - struments play, To ce - le-brate, to ce - le-brate this tri - um-phant day;

Tune all your voi - ces, and in - stru-ments play, To ce - le-brate, to ce - le-brate this

Tune all your voi - ces, and in - stru - ments play, To ce - le-brate, to ce - le-brate this

Tune all your voi - ces, and in - stru - ments play, To ce - le-brate, to ce - le-brate this

Tune all your voi - ces, and in - stru-ments play, To ce - le-brate, to ce - le-brate this

tri - um - phant day, To ce - le - brate, to ce - le - brate this tri - um - phant day.

tri - um - phant day, To ce - le - brate, to ce - le - brate this tri - um - phant day.

tri - um - phant day, To ce - le - brate, to ce - le - brate this tri - um - phant day.

tri - um - phant day, To ce - le - brate, to ce - le - brate this tri - um - phant day.

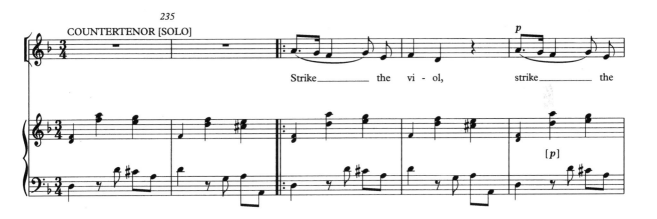

COUNTERTENOR [SOLO]

Strike_____ the vi - ol, strike_____ the

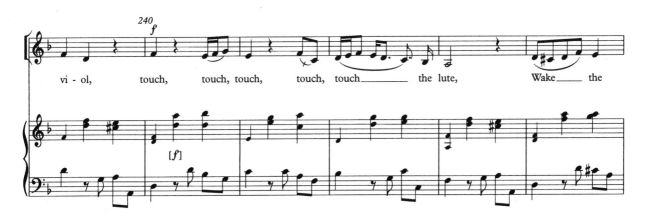

vi - ol, touch, touch, touch, touch, touch_____ the lute, Wake_____ the

harp, wake___ the harp, wake___ the harp, in - spire___ the

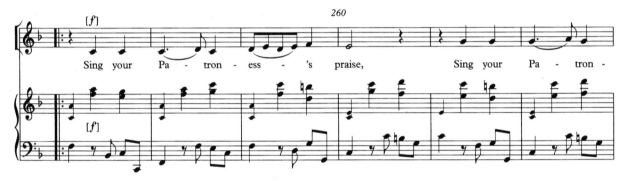

flute, Wake___ the harp, in - spire___ the flute; flute;

Sing your Pa - tron - ess - 's praise, Sing your Pa - tron -

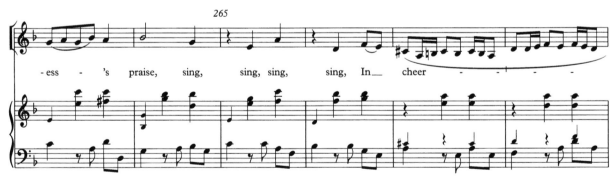

- ess - 's praise, sing, sing, sing, sing, In___ cheer - - - -

- - - - ful_ and har - mon - ious lays; lays.

BASS SOLO

The day that such a bless -

- ing gave No com-mon, com-mon fes - ti - val should be, No, no, no,

no, no, no, no com-mon fes - ti - val should be; be. What it

just - ly, what it just - ly, it just - ly seem'd to crave Grant, O

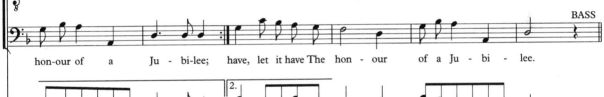

360

gave No com - mon, com-mon fes - ti - val should be, No, no, no, no,

gave No com - mon, com-mon fes - ti - val should be, No, no, no, no,

gave No com - mon, com-mon fes - ti - val should be, No, no, no,

gave No com - mon, com-mon fes - ti - val should be, No, no, no,

365

no, no, no com-mon fes - ti - val should be; The be.

no, no, no com-mon fes - ti - val should be; be.

no, no, no, no com-mon fes - ti - val should be; be.

no, no, no, no com-mon fes - ti - val should be; be.

What it just - ly, what it just - ly, it just - ly seem'd to

What it just - ly, what it just - ly, it just - ly seem'd to

What it just - ly, what it just - ly, it just - ly seem'd to

What it just - ly, what it just - ly, it just - ly seem'd to

crave　Grant, O grant,　grant, O grant, and let it

crave　Grant, O grant,　grant, O grant, and let it

crave　Grant, O grant,　grant, O＿ grant, and let it

crave　Grant, O grant,　grant, O grant, and let it

SOPRANO SOLO

Bid the Vir - tues, bid the Gra - - - ces, bid the Gra-ces to the sa - - - - - - - - cred shrine__ re - - pair, Round_____ the al - tar take, take__ their pla - - ces, round_____

the al - tar take,_____ take_____ their pla - ces, Bless-ing with re - turns_____ of

pray'r, Bless-ing with re - turns_____ of pray'r Their great_____ De-fen-der's care, Their great,_____

_____ their great_____ De-fen-der's care, While Ma-

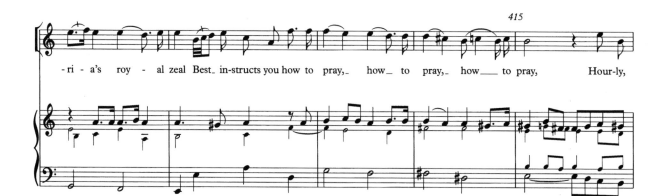

- ri - a's roy - al zeal Best_ in-structs you how to pray,_ how_ to pray,_ how_ to pray, Hour-ly,

hour-ly from her own   Con-vers-ing,   con-vers-ing,   con-vers-ing with th' E - ter -

- nal,   the E - ter - nal_ Throne.

BASS SOLO

These,   these,   these are the sa-cred

charms,   these are the sa-cred charms that shield   Her dar - - - - - ing

He-ro in— the field, These, these are the sa-cred charms, These are the sa-cred charms that

shield Her dar - - - - - ing He-ro in— the field, Her

dar - - - - - ing He-ro in— the— field: Thus she sup -

-ports_____ his— right-eous cause, Thus, thus, thus, thus,

_____ to his aid im-mor - - - - - tal pow'r she draws.

[VERSE]
SOPRANO

See Na-ture, re - joic-ing, has shown us_ the way With in-no-cent re-vels, with in-no-cent

BASS

See Na-ture, re - joic-ing, has shown us_ the way With in-no-cent re-vels, with in-no-cent

re-vels to wel-come the_ day; See day. The tune - ful_ grove and talk - ing rill, The

re-vels to wel-come the day; See day. The tune - ful_ grove and talk - ing rill, The

laugh - ing vale, re - ply - ing hill, With charm - ing har - mo - ny___ u - nite, The

laugh - ing vale, re - ply - ing hill, With charm - ing har - mo - ny u - nite, The

hap - py sea - son to in - vite. Thus Na - ture, re - joic-ing, has shown us___ the way With

hap - py sea - son to in - vite. Thus Na-ture, re - joic-ing, has shown us___ the way With

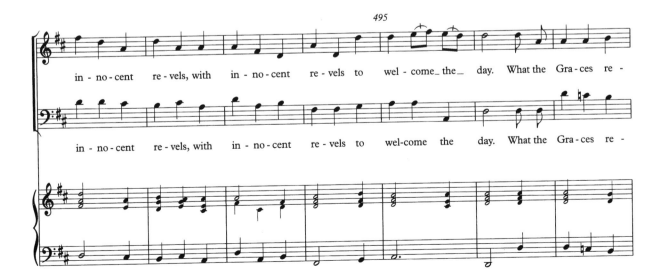

in - no - cent re - vels, with in - no - cent re - vels to wel - come___ the___ day. What the Gra - ces re -

in - no - cent re - vels, with in - no - cent re - vels to wel-come the day. What the Gra - ces re -

re-vels to wel-come_the_ day; See Na-ture, re - joic-ing, has shown us_ the way With

re-vels to wel-come the day; See Na-ture, re - joic-ing, has shown us the way With

re-vels to wel-come the day; See Na-ture, re - joic-ing, has shown us the way With

re-vels to wel-come the day; See Na-ture, re - joic-ing, has shown us_ the way With

in - no-cent re - vels, with in - no-cent re - vels to wel - come_the_ day. The tune - ful_

in - no-cent re - vels, with in - no-cent re - vels to wel-come the day. The tune - ful

in - no-cent re - vels, with in - no-cent re - vels to wel-come the day. The tune - ful_

in - no-cent re - vels, with in - no-cent re - vels to wel-come the day. The tune - ful_

grove and talk - ing rill, The laugh - ing vale, re - ply - ing hill, With

grove and talk - ing rill, The laugh - ing vale, re - ply - ing hill, With

grove and talk - ing rill, The laugh - ing, the laugh - ing vale, re - ply-ing hill, With

grove and talk - ing rill, The laugh - ing vale, re - ply - ing hill, With

charm - ing har - mo - ny___ u - nite, The hap - py sea - son to in -

charm - ing har - mo - ny u - nite, The hap - py sea - son to in -

charm - ing har - mo - ny___ u - nite, The hap - py sea - son to___ in -

charm - ing har - mo - ny u - nite, The hap - py sea - son to in -

550 ... 555

-vite. Thus Na-ture, re-joic-ing, has shown us the way With in-no-cent re-vels, with

560

in-no-cent re-vels to wel-come the day. What the Gra-ces re-quire, And the Mu-ses in-

Printed and bound in Great Britain by
Caligraving Limited Thetford Norfolk